TURN THANKS

Turn Thanks
Poems by Lorna Goodison

UNIVERSITY OF ILLINOIS PRESS

URBANA AND CHICAGO

Manufactured in the United States of America

P 5 4 3 2 1

♾ This book is printed on acid-free paper.

Library of Congress Cataloging-in-Publication Data
Goodison, Lorna.
Turn thanks : poems / by Lorna Goodison.
p. cm.
ISBN 0-252-06788-6 (acid-free paper)
1. Caribbean Area—Poetry.
2. Jamaica—Poetry.
I. Title.
PR9265.9.G6T87   1999
811—ddc21   98-25508
CIP

To Barbara Goodison Gloudon

and Ancile Gloudon

with special thanks to Keith Goodison

and Karl Goodison

and to my friends Wolfgang Binder

and Elaine Melbourne

Contents

PART 1

My Mother's Sea Chanty

After the Green Gown of My Mother Gone Down

August, her large heart slows down then stops.
Fall now, and trees flame, catch a fire and riot

last leaves in scarlet and gold fever burning.
Remember when you heard Bob Marley hymn

"Redemption Song," and from his tone and timbre
you sensed him traveling? He had sent the band home

and was just keeping himself company, cooling star,
sad rudeboy fretting on cowboy box guitar

in a studio with stray echo and wailing sound
lost singing scatting through the door of no return.

When the green goes, beloved, the secret is opened.
The breath falls still, the life covenant is broken.

Dress my mother's cold body in a deep green gown.
Catch a fire and let fall and flame time come

after the green gown of my mother gone down.

We laid her down, full of days,
chant griot from the book of life,
summon her kin from the long-
lived line of David and Margaret.
Come Cleodine, Albertha,
Flavius, Edmund, Howard and Rose,
Marcus her husband gone before
come and walk Dear Doris home.

And the Blue Mountains will open to her
to seal her corporeal self in.
From the ancient vault
that is their lapis lazuli heart
the headwaters of all our rivers spring.
Headwaters, wash away the embalmer's myrrh resin
the dredging of white powder caking her cold limbs.

Return her ripe body clean
to fallow the earth.
Her eyes to become brown agate stones.
From her forehead let there dawn
bright mornings.
May her white hair contribute
to the massing of clouds

cause the blood settled in her palms
to sink into fish-filled lagoons.
Earth, she was a mother like you
who birthed and nursed her children.
Look cherubims and angels, see her name
written down in the index of the faithful
in the mother-of-pearl book of saints.

Mama, Aunt Ann says
that she saw Aunt Rose
come out of an orchard
red with ripe fruit
and called out laughing to you.
And that you scaled the wall
like two young girls
scampering barefoot among
the lush fruit groves.

My Mother's Sea Chanty

I dream that I am washing
my mother's body in the night sea
and that she sings slow
and that she still breathes.

I see my sweet mother
a plump mermaid in my dreams
and I wash her white hair
with ambergris and foaming seaweed.

I watch my mother under water
gather the loose pearls she finds,
scrub them free from nacre
and string them on a lost fishing line.

I hear my dark mother
speaking sea-speak with pilot fish,
showing them how to direct barks
that bear away our grief and anguish.

I pray my mother breaks free
from the fish pots and marine chores
of her residence beneath the sea,
and that she rides a wild white horse.

The Domestic Science of Sunday Dinner

There is the soaking of the peas; the red kidney beans
dried out from hard life, which need to be revived
through the water process, overnight osmosis.

There is the seasoning of the meat
always with garlic which you scrape
with the serrated edge of an Okapi knife.

Mince these cloves of pungent flavor
then slice the circular onions, weeping
add the savor of salt and the bite of pepper,

add pimento kernels if you want and judicious
cut confetti of hot country pepper,
rub all this in with clean bare hands.

Your efforts will return to you
as aromas of contentment, harbingers of feasting
and well-being on Sunday afternoon.

I learned how to prepare Sunday dinners
the August when my father was found to be housing
agressive cells of destruction within him,

cells which were even now massing for the final
battle against his system, which they would win
in the closing days of the Advent season.

"Put the peas on after breakfast," my mother said,
turning her domain, the kitchen, over to me
so that she could become his nurse at the end.

Their cooking requires close careful attention,
no long water will do, just enough to cover
and cook them till they sink to the bottom.

Then add enough water to buoy them again.
It's a game, this cooking of the peas.
Sometimes you allow them to cook down

until they almost burn. It is that cooked-down
near-burned state which produces that taste
of redeemed and rescued richness.

Repeat this boiling process over and over
until the hard red legumes soften.
Some of them will break open early

provided you do not cook them with salt.
The salt you add later when all peas have softened.
Flavor them again with more pressed garlic pearls.

Add the stripped length of stalks of escallion
pounded to release the onion brother juices.
Now toss a fragrant bouquet of thyme

into the swirling red waters of the pot,
which is even now awaiting the wash,
the white tide of coconut milk.

This part of the Sunday dinner ceremony
in times earlier was conducted by my father,
who would be summoned to the kitchen

and handed the instruments for performing
this ritual. A hammer, a knife, an ice pick,
a dry coconut bristling with fibrous hairs,

a male coconut in need of a shave
whose one eye you pierced with the ice pick's tip
to release a cloudy white fluid.

My father pauses to pour the water
into a long-stemmed wine glass
and lifts it like a chalice to my mother's lips.

Then he turns from this tender holy
and gallant gesture and splits open
the head of the coconut with the hammer.

The shell of the coconut cracks loudly
and opens to reveal that inside its thick skull
it is cradling a lining of firm white meat.

My father uses the blade of the knife
to separate the flesh from the shell,
and then he symbolically dips

a jagged piece of coconut into sugar
and chews upon it. This signals
the ending of this high domestic ceremony.

The coconut flesh is gathered up
and grated, then squeezed through a strainer.
The thick milk is tempered with water.

You pour that then like a libation
upon the seasoned red bubbling water
which is now ready to receive the rice,

clean sifted, picked, and washed
of all foreign bodies and impurities
like small pebbles and chaff

which remind us that all this is the produce,
the bounty of the earth into which
my father is preparing to return.

They come together, this integration
of rice and peas steamed in coconut milk,
mixed together and left to settle down

into a combined state of readiness.
All the time the meat has been roasting,
issuing from its side bloody gravy juices.

Now they will be serving her bland
hospital food, spiceless meat, mashed potatoes
accompanied by pastel vegetables.

This pale repast will be attended
by a nervous mound of red gelatin
and an eye cup of anemic ice cream.

They will encourage her to eat this
and to be thankful upon this Sunday
that at eighty-five she still lives.

For somedays she can only feed
upon an essential mixture, an imitation
plasma of salt sugar and water

dripping into her veins through a long
winding serpentine tube.
Over and over I watch for signs

that hearts are softening
that hard things are breaking open
that in the end it will all come together

like the Sunday dinner rice and peas.
As I pray for your soul's safety Mother,
as I pray for your blessed release.

Turn Thanks to Miss Mirry

Turn thanks to Miss Mirry
ill-tempered domestic helper who hated me.
She said that she had passed through hell bareheaded
and that a whitening ash from hell's furnace

had sifted down upon her and that is why she gray early.
Called me "Nana." Nanny's name I have come to love.
She twisted her surname Henry into Endry
in her railing against the graceless state of her days.

She was the repository of 400 years of resentment
for being uprooted and transplanted, condemned
to being a stranger on this side of a world
where most words would not obey her tongue.

She said that she came from "Ullava"
in the parallel universe of Old Harbor.
She could not read or write a word in English
but took every vowel and consonant of it

and rung it around, like the articulated neck
of our Sunday dinner sacrificial fowl.
In her anger she stabbed at English, walked it out,
abandoned it in favor of a long kiss teeth,

a furious fanning of her shift tail, a series of hawks
at the back of her throat, a long extended elastic sigh,
a severing cut eye, or a melancholy wordless moaning
as she squatted over her wooden washtub soaping

our dirty clothes with a brown wedge of hard key soap.
To Miss Mirry who subverted the English language
calling Barbara, Baba; my father, Tata; who desiled her mind
that I was boofuttoo, a baffan and too rampify.

Who said pussbrukokonatinnadalikklegalnanayeye.
Miss Mirry versus English against the west
once assured me that for every sickness
there exists a cure growing in the bush.

I thank her for giving me a bath in her washtub
which she had filled with water heated
in a kerosene tin and in it she had strewed
the fringed leaves of the emancipation tamarind.

I turn thanks for the calming bath
that she gave to me which quelled effectively
the red itching measles prickling my skin.
As she sluiced the astringent waters over me

she was speak-singing in a language
familar to her tongue which rose unfettered
up and down in tumbling cadences, ululations
in time with the swift sopping motion of her hands,

becoming her true self
in that ritual bathing, that song.
Turn thanks now to Miss Mirry
African bush healing woman.

Turn Thanks to Grandmother Hannah

My grandmother Hannah aspired to sanctity
through the domestic vocation of laundering
the used, soiled vestments of the clergy
into immaculate and unearthly brightness.

She would wash, starch and smooth them
like the last few feet of the road to heaven
with a heavy self-heater iron, its belly blazing
with the harnessed energy of the coals of hell.

Every clergyman in St. Elizabeth's parish
would seek out her cleansing service.
Reclaiming that which seemed marked
for perdition was Hannah's holy gift.

Wine-stained altar cloths, once-chaste white albs
would rejoice, spotless, transfigured
to stand, redeemed under the resurrecting
power of grandmother Hannah's hands.

To be perfect in whatsoever you are called to do
is counted in heaven as sincere prayer.
My father's mother prayed through
laundering the garments used in temple service.

To my grandmother with the cleansing power
in her hands, my intention here is to give thanks
on behalf of any who have experienced within
something like the redemption in her washing.

Love Song for Great-Grandmother Leanna

With emancipation you married
a stout free Guinea man.
In your lawful estate
you cultivated ribbon cane.

On your paid-for property
wheeled your private sugar mill O.
You reaped from a deep grove
of fragment allspice pimento.

You fanned your ripe berries
out upon your raised and wide barbecue.
For a wedding gift he gave you
a tall-flanked gray mule.

You rode upon it like a backra missus,
sidesaddle or astride depending on the day.
Sidesaddle days were Sundays
you cantered into Lucea to social soirees.

You descended from the mule's height
in one swift fluid movement.
And if someone too familiar should forget
themself and call out, "Whoa Leanna"

you would turn and rebuke them,
"Say remember do, it is now Mrs. Buddle to you."

Aunt Rose's Honey Advice

My aunt Rose told me
that it is always good
for lovers to keep honey
mixed in with their food.

"Keep it around the house
at all times," she said.
Replace slick butter
with pure honey on bread.

Feed it to your love
from a deep silver spoon.
Throw open the curtains
draw free honey from the moon.

Use it to lend a gold glow
to wan lustreless skin.
Fold it into honey cakes,
drizzle it into honey drinks.

Add a satin honey glaze
to the matte surface of everydays.
Voices sing polished
with honey's burnishing.

Shall we then beloved
become keepers of bees,
invite an entire colony
of workers, drones and a queen

to build complex
multicelled wax cities
near our home by the sea?
Would that mean that salt

would be savoring
through our honey?
And you say, "What of it?"
and give me a kiss

flavored with honey
and sea-salt mix.
Integrated honey you say.
Kiss me again is what I say

because the salt in that kiss
could be the sting from old tears
and we need to make up
for all our honeyless years.

Hardanga the Lost Stitch

Hardanga the lost stitch jumped off the needle,
slid down the long length of thread,
slipped the knot at the thread end,
and hid in the cracks of the wooden floor.

Johnny cooper, johnny cooper,
the woman kneeling beat out a rhythm
with the club-shaped coconut brush.
Shine a floor until you see your face in it.

A shining red-oxide surface. Hardanga
abandoned the bodice of linen dresses
ornate, overworked like bureau doilies,
picotted with fine hand embroidery.

Left behind the moon and star stitch
and the intricate web with anancy
the trickster spiderman trapped in it.
Hardanga hardanga you gone O.

My mother taught dozens of women
to sew. She insisted that was a way
for them to earn a bread. Earn a bread
miss lady, and live independent.

Bobbin and shuttle, presserfoot,
if the tension's too tight it will draw
up the stitch. She sewed so
at her Singer, my mother sewed

her long shanks tilting at
the broad wrought iron pedal
turning the handle like a spindle.
No camel goes through the eye of a needle.

Sewing never made her rich
but it gave her a good name
for giving a good fit. You can tell
a fine seamstress by the shoulder's fit

by the settled set of the collar,
by the neatness of seams.
Many a pretty dress will deceive,
outward appearance all put together

while inside the seams bristle
close to the body, spring wild and furry.
Remember, hot needle bun thread
when you sew clothes in a hurry.

In search of Hardanga the lost stitch
to sew up your garment of victory,
to seam up the robes of righteous lovers,
to hem up the mouths of the bad mind forever.

Notes from My Mother's Village before the Village Got Light

In those times, she says, in October
tenth month of the calendar year
the 0 in the ten would become an opening
a funnel through which rain would pour.

Those times evening refused to wait its turn
but would bore afternoon down
and spread out itself early in the sky
and green things would be the same, overbearing.

All vegetation would multiply into thickness
and that would provide hiding for restless spirits
who wandered the village seeking resting places
in hearts ruinate, and soul's abandoned estate.

In those times, she says, her brother Howard
took ill and died from a sudden and nameless fever.
He went to Lucea and came home with his body burning.
All the river water could not cool the fatal furnace within.

My grandfather, she says, celebrated St. Patrick's Day
by drinking a puncheon of rum and playing the violin.
Colonial combination, rum and violin. O to hear him sing,
the Lake Isle of Innisfree now became Harvey River. Lucea.

All this observed by the Guinea woman
who bore him a blue-eyed high yellow child
whose loyalties were torn and divided
between mother Africa and a son of the British Empire.

She says these things happened before the village got light.
And if you think that afternoon was impatient those days
what to say about night? For one minute you would bend down
to heap another yam hill and your insides would be saying

it is four o'clock, broad daylight still and you look up to see night
drawing on his black trousers running across the sky.
All these thing, she said, used to happen in Harvey River
before the village named after her grandfather got light.

Domestic Incense

Just then, in that early afternoon,
I wanted to be that simple woman
who had cooked you Saturday soup

using all golden foods. Bellywoman
pumpkin, yellow yams, sweet potato,
carrots and deep ivory bones of beef.

I would bear it to you in an enamel bowl,
the smell of fragrant thyme and pimento
would waft, domestic incense, as I go.

How the hot Scotch Bonnet pepper
would issue its flavor through
the ripened walls of its own skin

but because like our love its seeds
can scorch, I'd be careful to remove it
before it cooked itself into breaking.

Signals from the Simple Life

A red cloth
tight around
her brow
and he knows
she is being
cleansed now
by the tides
of the moon.

White napkin
folded
over her sex
at death
is signal
to interfering spirits
she is done
with the ways of the flesh.

A poor man
wears new gloves
on his wedding day
to say
his hands
are clean.
This is
his new beginning.

PART 2
This Is My Father's Country

This Is My Father's Country

Yet when he died he did not own
one square inch of this rich red earth.
His body is interred in the churchyard
at Half Way Tree, far from his birthplace

eighty-seven miles from the wintergreen hills
of Malvern, the land his mother used to own,
well-fruited land, with the bearing Julie mango
tree, his navel string coiling at the roots.

My father's birthright was robbed
by a man whose intention it was
to store up much treasure here on earth.
A fox-name man stole my father's red land.

Sly Russell, you caught her in dry season.
Every crop that year had come to fail.
You caught Grandmother in the dry season,
her son sick with a fever there was no name for.

Grandmother, who never took her business
to strangers, in distress gave her land papers
to Russell to hold in exchange for a small sum,
six pounds to go and doctor her son.

The land papers stuck to Russell's fingers
and Grandmother received poor justice
when she appealed to King George
and his cohorts at Black River courthouse.

Her only recourse was to petition
St. Elizabeth, "St. Elizabeth come and see
this woman's dying trial, how I am left
with no red land of my own to walk upon,

to walk upon and raise my dumb animals,
to cultivate my crops, to will to my son.
I will lay down and die and be buried
under land that is not my own.

St. Elizabeth, make tiefing Russell unable
to take my children's birthright with him.
May they use it as a loose red blanket
to cover him in his suit of cedar board.

St. Elizabeth pray for my generations.
St. Elizabeth please pray for my children's
children, pray for all of us who are not able
to store up treasures here on earth.

St. Elizabeth, you who changed
the bread of the poor into roses
and then converted the roses
into the bread of the poor again,

grant us consoling strength
to bear our wounds and losses
and transform our sufferings
like the bread and the roses."

II

This is my father's country
and of late I have been thinking
how the burnished copper of his skin
could mean that he was Amerindian.

And as I write this I swear I see him smiling.

Like Arawak, my father did not come to stay.
His temper blazed sudden like bamboo fire
to be quickly dispersed by the wind
no traces of bitterness remaining.

My father of the tribe who came singing.

The earth is red here on the Pedro Plains
veils of rain mist shroud the trees, vapor
like winding sheets around Spur Tree Hill.
I hear now my spirit father, raconteur,

tell how it could take nights and days
for trucks to ascend these treacherous slopes.
How a Fargo would roll back like Sisyphus's stone
until the driver and sidemen effected the system,

called the cotching of the wheel. Advance a little,
cotch it with a stone, the recommended
way of advancement over any treacherous road.
Beloved, all the way here the roads ran red.

We cotched wheels, we stopped and waited,
eating of the round loaf, watching the waters
drench the fields, parched and unaccustomed
to wet they swallow hard and drink too fast.

In these parts, farmers have been known
to set straw traps to catch the morning dew.
In that way they moisten the roots of escallion
thyme, onion, potato, peas and sweet cassava.

Irrigation by grace and cultivation through
perseverance. Now for our coming, abundance.
Today there is torrential, overflowing blessing.
From my father's country drive away all drought.

The sight of your clean hands
breaking the bread
is turning my heart inside out.

My sweet-foot father could dance you see,
my nightingale-throat father could sing,
wind and string instruments obeyed him.

Here is a rude song he taught me
a ribald ditty, about the false candy
found by the village simpleton
and sung to one Bredda Manny.

Bredda Manny o mi fine a candy
Bredda Manny o mi fine a candy
dash it wey you nasty bitch
you nasty bitch, a puss shit.

Compose now a song for my father,
a man with well-shaped feet,
high-arched insteps for a man.
My father Marcus was a dandy.

A clean man who changed his shirts
often
Of Sea Island cotton in the Tower Isle
style
stood screened upon a background of white,

red-seamed Policemen upon point duty.
At regular intervals spring coconut trees,
recurring royally in between these
is the regal tower motif.

III

They say that if you dream your father
and he does not speak that is an ill omen.
And I dream my father, he does not speak,
he does not speak, there is no need.

He smiles so and the room is filled
with stillness, high transcendent peace.
One Christmas I spent in New York alone
my father appeared to me on Dry Harbor Road.

He burst through the doors of the funeral home
and rapidly ascended the fire escape
then hovered as a bright ball of light
illuminating my solitary actions at evening.

He hovered outside in the snow
glowing over the music issuing out the window,
he and I serenaded by his favorite singer,
Harry Belafonte, crooning "Jamaica Farewell"

and "Shenandoah" and "Sleep Late My Lady Friend."

Song of My Great-Grandfather William

My great-grandfather William
was a seeker who caught the silence.
He nursed it within him till it bloomed
into a candleflower in his chest.

He was a tall big-boned man.
The earth shuddered under his steps
but the caught-quiet at his center
pulled peace to him like a strong magnet.

When his frail wife Lily expired
he took great-grandmother Nana as bride.
She who served them as faithful maid.
His gesture compensated for Hagar's shame.

He married her in the parish church
at Lucea for all the scandalized backra
to see. She served him to the end as maid,
faithful maid become well married.

My Uncle

When my uncle died
he had daughters and sons
enough to bear his coffin
sufficient to lay him out.

One was a carpenter.
He built a fine casket
planed it from the trunk
of a fragrant cedar tree

that grew high as if heading
up to heaven ahead of uncle
lofty in his front yard
for the best part of a century.

One was a stone mason.
He constructed the vault.
While he was underground
he smoothed out a second tomb

for the pious wife of my uncle
who to this day still lives
on the nourishment pressed
from thin bible leaves.

His daughters, fine seamstresses,
lined his coffin with purple.
They washed and dressed him
in a serge suit of dark blue.

He'd cut and stitched it himself.
He was a tailor and farmer
with a gift in his hands
for good fit and perfect lucea yams.

His family fed all who came
to help them mourn
with the flesh of his goats
and ground provisions of his land.

I dreamt I saw my uncle
entering the Jubilee pavilion of Kings.
Osiris weighed his heart against a feather
and his heart was not found wanting.

The Sleeping Zemis

He kept the zemis under his bed for years
after the day he came upon them in a cave
which resembled the head of a great stone god,
the zemis placed like weights at the tip of its tongue.

Arawaks had hidden them there when they fled,
or maybe the stone god's head was really a temple.
Now under his bed slept three zemis,
wrought from enduring wood of ebony.

The first was a man god who stood erect, his arms
folded below his belly. The second was a bird god
in flight. The third was fashioned in the form
of a spade, in the handle a face was carved.

A planting of the crops zemi,
a god for the blessing of the corn,
for the digging of the sweet cassava
which requires good science

to render the white root safe food.
And over the fields the john crows wheel
and the women wait for the fishermen
to return from sea in boats hollowed from trees.

Under his bed the zemis slept.
Where were they when Columbus
and his men, goldfever and quicksilver
on the brain, came visiting destruction?

Man god we gave them meat, fish and cassava.
Silent deity we mended their sails, their leaking
ships, their endless needs we filled even with
our own lives, our own deaths.

Bird god, we flew to the hills,
their tin bells tolling the deaths
of our children, their mirrors
foreshadowing annihilation to follow.

Spade god we perished.
Our spirits wander wild and restless.
There was no one left to dig our graves,
no guides to point us the way to Coyaba.

He turned them over to the keepers of history,
they housed them in glass-sided caves.
Then he went home to sleep without the gods
who had slumbered under his bed for years.

Africa on the Mind Today

Over the wall the workmen chant
riding the rhythm hammer on nail
beating out a one-drop that will not
be forgotten after four hundred years.

Rounding a corner in Green Island
by the restless cobalt sea at evening
a line of young men run in formation
like warriors at the hunt of the lion.

Africa on the mind today.
The workmen drumming over the wall
call to Miriam singing Sangoma
sing a "do not destroy" for Winnie Mandela.

Sing a Bide-Up for Wole Soyinka
say, Abeocuta rock of our foreparents stay.
Strength of Guinea women on our mother's side,
Africa rest, Abeocuta abide.

Nana Yah, Your Teacher

Upon those slow mornings
and drowsing afternoons
when you would levitate
off the wooden benches

in cathedral-ceilinged classrooms
Grandy Nanny would signal
with a tinnin mirror from the mountains
blinding your mind to dead knowledge.

She taught you the out-of-body trick.
Look interested, arrange a stare, fix it.
Gather yourself and exit through
the eye between your eyes.

At play in the African star grass
you fed upon wild bush grapes which
when pressed yielded maroon wine,
not the pale-vintage Trevelyan kind.

For botany she bid you study
the violet-crowned lignum vitae,
mathematics and science formulae
she transmitted through drum-speak.

And then there were the life lessons
in stealth. Observe how guinea grass
matched your uniform dress; reenter and wait
on the day of Jubilee to rise and reveal yourself.

About Almonds and Ambergris

There is a perfume rising off the sea today.
A scent of almond top notes and base notes of ambergris.

I think about ambergris, a griege ball of scent starter
coiled in the stomach of sperm whales or rolling free,

a pomander perfuming the waters of oceans.
Did Jonah know that he was valuable as ambergris

sought after and needed to touch pulse points?
I meditate upon these matters this day as I lie

upon the outer reaches of Lysson's Beach.
I think that I shall add the scent of berries now

to the perfume rising off the ocean. Water berries,
bright red such as those which cheered the eyes of Columbus

when he feared the sea would dip under and that he christopher
and his colombo in the Nina the Pinta and the Santa Maria

would be drawn down to the weed-clogged seafloor.
O Christobal Colun set out for Cipangu and China

sweet winds swept his caravelles out to sea,
blessed weather, April month in Andalusia.

Now three ships full of frightened men
who have crossed that fine line of foam

into uncharted waters. Then Christobal sights
carved board horses and green branches

fresh branches semaphoring berries, life cast upon water.
There is a sweet smell coming off the sea today

of almonds and ambergris and red berries.
I think about Columbus and how he thought at first

these islands would be a source of gold,
of cotton and mastic, aloes, wood, and things invaluable

to him, poor thing. That sweet smell rising off the sea today.
May the perfumed tides wash my people now bright berries.

PART 3
The Mango of Poetry

The Mango of Poetry

I read a book
about the meaning of poetry.
The writer defines it as silence,
then breaks the lines

to construct ideas
about the building of bridges,
the reconciliation of opposites.
I'm still not sure what poetry is.

But now I think of a ripe mango
yellow ochre niceness
sweet flesh of St. Julian,
and all I want to do

is to eat one from the tree
planted by my father
three years before the sickness
made him fall prematurely.

The tree by way of compensation
bears fruit all year round
in profusion and overabundance
making up for the shortfall

of my father's truncated years.
I'd pick this mango with a cleft stick,
then I'd wash it and go to sit
upon the front wall of our yard.

I would not peel it all back
to reveal its golden entirety,
but I would soften it by rolling
it slowly between my palms.

Then I'd nibble a neat hole
at the top of the skin pouch
and then pull the pulp
up slowly into my mouth.

I'd do all this while wearing
a bombay-colored blouse
so that the stain of the juice
could fall freely upon me.

And I say that this too would be
powerful and overflowing
and a fitting definition
of what is poetry.

To Mr. William Wordsworth, Distributor of Stamps for Westmoreland

The host of golden flowers at my feet
were common buttercups not daffodils,
they danced and swayed so in the breeze
though overseer thorns were planted among them.

Still, it was a remarkable show of sorts
which opened my eye, the inward one,
which once opened enabled me to see
the overflowing bounty of my peoples' poverty.

Sir, did you pass my great-grandmother?
Like you she lived in Westmoreland,
she rode upon a great gray mule,
she could not read or write, she did not buy stamps.

But great-grandmother was a poet
who wrote her lyrical ballads on air,
scripted them with her tongue
then summoned them to return to her book of memory.

She never did arrange them
the exact same way twice
but they were her powerful overflow
recollected in tranquility, sir, what she chanted was poetry.

Great-grandmother was Black Betty's daughter,
sister to fool fool Rose, distant cousin
to Betty Foy's idiot boy. Laughingstock
of the West Country, of no degree, she spoke funny.

But, sir, whenever she would sing
even the solitary reaper's voice was stilled
as her wild mystic chanting issued
over the cane brakes and hills. Only Keats's nightingale

could compete with her guinea griot style.
But she was not in any contest
for the fittest of the fit, she just come
with her wild ways to enchant with her riddling lyrics.

Mr. Wordsworth, I am not buying any stamp
to post a letter to my great-grandmother.
She is a denizen of the spirit world like you
so I am asking you when you pass her there, to tell her

that I collected up all her songs and poems
from where they fell on banana trash.
The binding ones on the star apple tree,
the ones hidden like pound notes under her coir mattress.

I rescued them, rat-cut Blue Mountain coffee
the ratoon and dunder ones, refuse and trash
of the sugarcane, the ones they call broken
and indecent, patois, bungo, words for bondage and shame.

And I've written them down for her,
summoned them to stand, black-face type
against a light background, Mr. Wordsworth.
Please tell Miss Leanna her poems are now written down.

Country, Sligoville

I arise and go with William Butler Yeats
to country, Sligoville
in the shamrock green hills of St. Catherine.

We walk and palaver by the Rio Cobre
till we hear tributaries
join and sing, water songs of nixies.

Dark tales of Maroon warriors,
fierce women and men
bush comrades of Cuchulain.

We swap duppy stories, dark night doings.
I show him the link of a rolling calf's chain
and an old hige's salt skin carcass.

Love descended from thickets of stars
to light Yeats's late years with dreamings
alone I record the mermaid's soft keenings.

William Butler, I swear my dead mother
embraced me. I then washed off my heart
with the amniotic water of a green coconut.

In December Sally water will go down
to the Sally gardens with her saucer
and rise and dry her weeping orbs.

O to live, Inisfree, in a house of wattle and daub.

Moon Cakes and Anna Akhmatova

Cold Sundays are Russian tea cake days,
shaped like full and crescent moons they are.

Their crisp surface lightly dusted with snow
white sugar or icing powder of stars.

Embedded in their smooth lunar flesh
is the poppy seed fallout from poet planets.

And I think of Anna Akhmatova
as I have tea in my small room.

How her willow-slender figure settled
into black dresses and stoutness,

and her angular profile rounded, as she spent
her last days in a small room writing winter poems.

Cold Sunday, I imitate Anna Akhmatova
writing poems, eating of solitary cakes

in this blue Ann Arbor room,
cakes cut from full and harvest moons.

Antoinette Cosway Explains

It was always this way.
A morning breeze passing
could bruise my cheek.
The white zest of jasmine
trailed indoors by the night wind
would settle itself upon my skin
then conduct its essence down
into my blood, causing my body
to swarm and my head to spin.

Everything that I saw
was stirred up so,
wild cocoa leaves
became at once menacing masks.
Helaconia blooms were totemic staffs.
The inverted bell-mouth of angel trumpet
flowers would come to resemble
the turned-down cups of bitter port
drunk by fallen angels.

It was always so.
Standing in sunshine a cooler sun
would appear and direct its rays down
to render me cold.
The warm waters of the bathing pool
never refreshed but chilled me.
Sent me shivering to sit
on a warm white stone
which at my touch turned cool.

And the stone-heart girl,
the stone-heart girl
stole my good dress,
my friendship,
my bright pennies.
I hear counter-music
under all music,
no matter how they play
piano, piano.

I hear the streeling of Gypsy fiddles
of Gaelic choirs keening burial songs
just when the same destructive man
(he comes in different disguises
but he is the same man)
places his slow hand low
upon the small of my back and then
tilts my head back to begin again
the go-round go-round dance of death.

Song of the Burnt Gypsy of the City of Erlangen

Her husband is an artist.

He paints upon her skin
with a tempera that he himself
has mixed, grinding blocks
of color which he blends
with egg albumen.

He stays within the ochre range.
Burnt sienna for her.
He wakes at dawn,
stretches her flat
like a warm canvas,

then masterfully
he paints upon her.
Always the same painting.
Painting of a Gypsy woman
with scorched face and limbs.

His impasto perfectly
laid down is so convincing
that horrified citizens,
conscience stricken,
shower her with alms,

averting their eyes
from her caramelized skin.
Her husband is an artist.
She is his masterpiece.
Everyday he recreates the
same painting.

The Gypsy in the Russian Tea Room

The Gypsy in the Russian Tea Room
nests in a banquette like a fat firebird
with brocaded plumage. Her scarlet
and black tasseled scarf drips silk feathers
upon the figured carpet. At the center
of her forehead is fixed a silver eye,
the soothsayer's outward sign.

This man and woman in the Russian
Tea Room could tell the Gypsy
tales about cataclysm and misfortune.
Advise her how to dodge the fallout
from exploding planets and malevolent
constellations. They could sell her charms
to protect her when the conjunction of Mars

and treacherous women and venal men
means take low and keep silent, till scorpion
planets consume themselves. They do not want
their fortunes told. She has already bought
hers from the wandering wine-seller. His was
concealed in the purple grapes upon which he feeds.
Their fortune is to drink the mixed wine of destiny.

Vincent and the Orient

The blackbird in the bougainvillea bush
brushes against the powder blue sky.
The carnelian froth of the flowering tree,
and the way that this picture
framed itself inside my window,

makes me remember again Vincent
and the Orient he would imitate,
japonaiserie, white-petaled trees
set spare in an Eastern landscape.
They are not my favorite. Dearer to me

are those in which familiar things turn
transcendent. Golden cornfields
shimmy like blonde dancing girls,
hips rolling, abandoned, fecund.
The red turban of a zouave's uniform

pulsing like a live internal organ.
Strange how I never meditate upon
the harsh details of his death
but see instead the glory of his gift
for transforming elementary things

through patience and careful seeing
past all obvious appearances
down to where the whirling spirits
flash primal pigments, creating
images, sensuous, duende, amazing.

Letter to Vincent Van Gogh

Whether you will receive this letter or not I cannot tell.
Still, I intend to send it,
because it seems that like you, I'm driven to do things
which nobody encourages me to do.
No one was drawn by the smoke issuing from your chimney
like the sheer floating scarf of a Parisian woman
waving good-byes that were really invitations.
Nobody much coming or going to see you, to inquire after your views,
to spend the night under your red coverlet, to stay for soup.
For then you could have shown them your sunflowers
and your night skies.
Your gold sun spinning in the holy blue skies over
your canvases at Arles.
I write now to confirm that the blue of your irises
can only be described as themselves.
That the urgency of your brush strokes recorded the accelerated
spinnings of this earth.
This took place so subtly that only eighty-eight souls here below
detected that all things now turn faster.
It seems that at the very moment that these increased
revolutions began, your brush strokes intensified.
Then too, it is now clear that it was you who penetrated
the mystery of gold.
You saw how it had its origins in the sun, how gold on earth
is really imitation.
You found it useful for lighting wheatfields and dyeing daffodils
and to thin it with longing as a medium to wash the walls of your room.
The medium of longing, the golden hope exploding across the
wheatfields with crows,
harsh crows who came finally calling.

Vincent, last evening when the moon was on full there was seen
off-center in the sky a new and brilliant constellation,
your name picked out in stars in the fixed heavens.
Stars of forbearance. Galaxy of endurance.
Vincent, true and magic alchemist, this is your constellation.
A company of stars dedicated to you,
who give light to dreamers who create and weep
and recreate and wait their turn and savor their salt and weep.

Sincerely,
Amber, dreamer

Max Ernst Painting

This floating woman without a head
her left arm missing.
The woman wearing one translucent
pink stocking
levitates in a blue space, rags and feathers
shudder from vents in the ceiling.

Someone just threw a stone at her.
See it drop to the base of the picture.
Maybe it was the stone that decapitated her.
There is a conical red stroke falling
from an indigo mass below
where the rags and feathers blow.

This woman with her head gone
she is partly a nun, partly naked maja.
Her left arm connected to her heart
grew weary of constantly reaching out
and returning empty it fell into the sea.
About her head. You know how I said
it was severed by a stone?
I suspect it was thrown by someone
who had no sins they wished to speak of.

The Jerboa of John Dunkley

A jerboa logo on shoe polish tin
leaps its way into Barber's vision
it settles into his dream life
and becomes his own icon.

Barber what a razor's edge
you walked, walking your razor
through the curled lamb's wool
of the head of the Negro.

As you barber you are called to stain
your chair with primodial images.
Jerboa dancing in the barber mirror
made you shut up shop that day

it yielded hairs for brush bristles
and you covered the canvas with gray.
"When I paint I take a walk," you confessed
to the keeper of dreams, Philip,

and then you showed him your painting
of a lone being in the Bog Walk gorge
observing a dark horse and buggy
go past rocky roads of miry clay.

Draw deep from your palette somber,
pure palette brooding chiaroscuro.
Dark greens and silver, muted
like the voice of the sing-slow Barber.

Down the winding rabbit hole
through the door of no return
Barber reclaims original landscape,
blue road ribbons to Port of Al Mina.

Marsupial jerboa leaps from shoe polish tin
blue rabbit roots at banana tree
when Barber takes a walk down the road
of captured collective memory.

Hungry Belly Kill Daley

I fancied that I could paint
a still life with food,
and my rendering of victuals
would be so good
that I could reach into the canvas
and eat and fill my belly.

Cadmium yellow could spread
butter impasto over white lead
or a brown loaf baked of sienna.
Scarlet and vermilion, the wine
would flow, otaheiti apple
is a deep, dark, rose madder.

If I could fill my hungry belly
with painted wine and bread
but they shock my visions from my head
at Bellevue, where Louis Q. Bowerbank
sends madmen or black men mad enough
to think that we could be artists, in 1940.

To Become Green Again and Young

In Rio de Janiero
they go at midnight
to welcome the new year.

Fresh in white garments
bearing white candles
they assemble by the sea

to toss old year's errors
griefs and mistakes
into the accepting waves.

Begin again fresh and new
when the year turns to become
green again and young.

Would there was a body of water
deep and wide enough
for the errors of some of us.

Arctic, Antarctic, Atlantic, Indian, Pacific
Caribbean Sea, Atlantic Ocean
where our ancestors drowned.

There is a spirit nation
under the ocean. May its citizens plead
for our recovery and redemption.

Midnight at the close of this year,
ancestral spirits urge us
to entrust our sorrows to the sea.

PART 4

God a Me

God a Me

Tide wash me out of the river
sweep me up onto the bank.

I was swimming in sync
so with the live currents

of the big rivers, one hundred
rivers of this green island.

Now here I am beached
but still breathing.

They say I'm the only one
who can live so

outside of the water culture
where fish flourish and grow.

Fish out of water
God a me

Fish live on land
God a me

Slightly amphibian
God a me

My name itself a prayer
God a me

On land I breathe uneasy
but still breathe though

until the tides of mercy
pull me

back into
the flow.

God a me.

Sometimes on a Day Such as This

Sometimes on a day such as this
after four or five hours
of medicinal silence
I am eased to this place.

I return home to myself,
clean, stripped. I enter
through the high blue door
of myself. I sit.

Within this chamber
of myself
loving you is as high a pleasure
as I will ever get.

See now my expanded self
grow many arms,
like a Hindu deity they issue
from my sides.

On cue, connected, I glow.
I become a living chandelier
swinging slightly with delight
because now you will pass beneath me

and one of my many lit fingers
will thoughtfully circle the crown
of your head.
And it will glow, halo.

Inside me I am never ashamed,
I am whole and me.
One thousand errors, transmuted
errors, now become iron

fed back into my blood.
I can hear a strong coursing
through my veins in the silence.
In the silence my blood runs

like the Tiber or the Black River.
My body contains a body
of strong surging water.
And I can hear it

sometimes on a day such as this
when I return home to me
after five hours or so
of medicinal silence.

When I Know You as Mountain

When I know you as mountain
you run liquid and ocean.
Sight you up as sun god
night calls your name moon.

You have exploded across
my understanding as rockets,
meteors, comets and shooting stars.
Last night you were moon again.

Now here you are, my morning star.
Before you turn your face
as final and fiery sunset
I beg to see you as tenderness.

On Houses

You ruined every house
that I ever built.
Turned me out
to roam the streets
of the universe.

Come winter I wear
a beggar's
ashen skin
and inch my way
across thin ice

fearful that I will fall
through a hole
in Ann Arbor
and land in marginally
colder Antarctica.

I settle lightly,
make no camp
no pagoda.
Your message
is clear enough.

This world is not
my home.
Old women moan
that sankey so,
fall hard upon
each note.

I dream of houses
built upon rocks
and yearn to live
inside them.
Till then
I fix flowers
in the open.

A Bed of Mint

A bed of mint
beneath the window
of the room where we sleep
will render the morning air
sharp and sweet.

I'd turn to you in my sleep
half out of dreams
murmuring "Whose bed
is it that smells of mint?"
"Ours" you will whisper.

Then we will roll over
like the waves and wake
to draw tea from the source
springing beneath the window.
Living sweet and sharp to each other.

Outwaiting the Crazy Wolf Moon

In the North the native people
call this the moon when wolves go crazy.
Here they warn against gathering bamboo
and wiss at the time of the full moon's rising.

For that is when the larvae swarm
in bamboo joints and wiss is alive with insects.
You will find that you have gathered
a bundle of useless sticks, sick with parasites.

It is wise to wait for the rise of the moon
called the moon of glad to be alive.
Soon after will follow the moon of new life,
the benevolent one which presides over

the ice melting, the earth thawing.
Here it is when resurrection lilies bloom
by the walls of penitentiaries,
burst out sudden from the cracks in tombs,

bloom straight up from the ground
in the small yards of faithful lovers
who learn strict patience and outwait
the mad moon of the crazy wolves.

I Know I Never Lose You

I know now that I never lose you.
Look how you came calling today
as thoughtful Sunday afternoon rain.

You in the making of the escoveitch,
onions, pepper, pimento, oil and vinegar,
for you all rejoice together.

Shiver the air then.
Combined condiments of praise,
you numinous in everdays.

Now strewn over the fatness
of fried butter fish,
behold bright thanksgiving garnish.

Like salt stirred evenly
into smooth food,
your presence permeates everything good.

Like oil in a cloth or dye
your substance imparted
changes the texture, the color of things.

You in all things, O everything,
all atoms saturated then
with your unction grace and presence.

Angel of Dreamers

Angel, ever since I come back here trying to reopen this dream shop
I get so much cuss-cuss and fight down, these merchants don't want me
to prosper in this town.

Seraph mine you supervised and trained me, inspected my goods
declared it celestial first quality. But cherubim what a cherubam
since I land.

I set up my shop in this big sprawling bazaar, central, to draw them
from near and from far. Well the first thing that I notice all around
and about me

is other sellers living in fear and under necromancy. Every morning
they get up they squeezing lime to cut and clear and all I using
is the power of prayers.

Some consulting with D lawrence (darkness) writing down my name on
parchment. Some have taken to attacking my name in malcrafted,
lopsided, imitations of my creations

all because of bad mind. Angel, if you see the spoil-goods they peddle
as dreamwares. Chuh, I leaving them to count the proceeds from their
bankruptcy sales.

For seraph, you should see how I fix up my shop, nobody around here
ever see a shop fix up like that. When I throw open the doors not even
the most bad-minded

could come out with their usual naysaying, carping and fault finding. For I have painted the walls in a deep evergreen, and all around the cornices and along the ceiling

I have picked out the subtle patterns in the mouldings in the indigo of discernment so what was hidden has now become clear, illuminate, and prominent.

Along the walls I have placed some long low cane-seat couches. The cushions all covered in the lavender of lignum vitae. It is there that dreamers sit and drink rosemary tea.

On the floor I dropped a rug of lagoon blue with feathers floating free on its surface, and if you look long and your eye is clear, you see schools of goldfish swimming down there.

And my extraordinary dreamshop was opened with no fanfare, not one high official, Pharisee or Tappanaris was there. I just threw open the doors and sat there quietly

till some dreamseeker pass by and noticed me. Someone well-parched from too much hard-heart life, they look up and see my sign a crescent moon with a single star fixed

and dreamseller lettered in font Gazelle, lower case, sans serif. And so they stumble in weary, having tried various health schemes and bush medicines and ask me for a dream.

As soon as they ask me I go to work like Attar, the darwish chemist, my ancestor. In a clean crucible I mix the fallout from stars and the fragrant dyestuff of roses.

I add to this, then, various elements for the restoration of lost shining. Only one or two hearts that have lived too long in the dark professed dissatisfaction with the dream they bought.

But most of the ones who acquire them always come back in to report how aquiring their dream has alchemically changed and altered their way of seeing and being.

They say to all visitors, "Come see this dream I have received from the seller in the bazzar, godchild of Ghazali, student of Attar, the love child of Rumi and Asi Itra.

One of the ancient keepers of dreams and songs, great granddaughter of a psalmist and griot Guinea woman. They say if you deserve one of these she will mix you one

to quicken your hopes and tune your heart to hear songs of bliss.
All she takes for payment is sincerity and red roses."
I have received many referrals in this way.

The ones who acquire these dreams are inspired to light candles of understanding which illuminate all they do thereafter with a clear pervasive shining.

I am writing this to you seated at the shop door where the simurgh, that cinnabar talisman of a bird, has just flown in and perched upon one of the bunches of wine-fruit

which hang ripe from the ceiling. Sometimes ground doves fly in and Barbary doves too. Let me attempt to describe the transcendent Barbary dove song for you.

The Trancendent Song as Taught by a Passing Tuareg Woman

A Tuareg woman passing once taught me a song.
It was really a series of intricate notes
urgently sounded, like the fast-forward call
of a rising flock of Barbary doves.

The song, if correctly and effectively done,
can lift me up to a cool place
above the burning chamber of the sun.
The woman said it is the transcendent song

known only to the ones like us.
I caught the song and held it.
I feel it is not wise to use it too frequently.
Just so, I have learned to save it for unbearable days.

First a series of fluttering notes
then a long low fluting coo.

Then a series of fast-forward notes
till there occurs a wild breakthrough.

Then a joyful, joyful gurgling
like a full-throttle rain replenished stream

and after that it's just pure sweet cooing.

The only way that I have been able to withstand
the undermining efforts of the other sellers
is to sound this transcendent song.

Until I see you face-to-face, I ask you to pray that God grant

me celestial insurance from the arsonist efforts
of the job-lot sellers.

I Have Spent These Snowbound Days
Away from Myself

I have spent these snowbound days away from myself
trying to inhabit a self that cannot now be me.

"Who am I?" I asked the woman that I was dressed in
and she, not knowing either, shrank back from her skin.

On these snowbound days all outside is an ice vista,
a frozen foreign landscape, a large acreage of white.

And some action, a sleight of hand working through this
persistent cold, has turned down the flow of my blood

so that it is icicling slowly in me. Now an ice shard
seems to have formed, it sharpens, it severs my heart.

I wake up to find my heart has left a red note, saying,
Gone in search of my identity, don't wait for me.

Who am I really? I have occasion to ask, as I walk past myself
each day. One girl said, "I don't think the tiger is you."

I agree, and I'm not the wild woman or Amber,
the Tightrope Walker, Penelope or the Mulatta.

Winter Dreams

I dream I am apprenticed to the master potter
the one who captured exactly the shade
of the eye shadow of Queen Nefertiti,
and spread it as Egyptian blue glaze
across the terra cotta surface
of a domestic water jar
so that it gleamed and became
a goblet fit for a Nubian queen.

I dream I am handmaid to the ancient of days,
that I'm drawing water from the Blue Nile river,
and when its waters rise and flood the banks
the potter who is now my father
regains youth and vigor
and rows me in a reed skiff past danger.

I lay down to sleep within my dream
clutching a semicircular vase
glazed in shades of damask rose.
Inscribed in raised letters
around its lip is the word "life."

Then I wake to snow over every surface
and more snow blowing. Unrelenting white
confetti from a veiled sky and my heart
still absent as I pass by myself.

You know, I have on occasion
offered my heart to some
who must have been utterly alarmed
at this raw, red, throbbing gift.

From afar it sometimes seems
like a rose, an artfully carved
and decorative rose, from overscarring
my heart has been carved into a rose.

About You and Me

Was it me that I found recently
in that cold sealed room
when the friction of our ways together
made sparks which caught at our center.
If I stand facing you will I see myself?

About Me

When I am supplicant,
prostrate and weeping,
sometimes I am lifted
up to source.

Source then turns me round
until I fall down exhausted.
My limbs realigned,
then I chant praises.

Treasure Beach

From Treasure Beach
the opaque black night
dropped across the horizon.
A fire cloth with a weighted hem.

I said, Here I wait until I am called in.
Then I passed over water
into these cities of ice
where I am still in waiting.

About Angels

I am sure that I met this angel before.
I think that in Benin we were married
and carried through streets of beaten gold
seated in elaborate wedding palanquins.

February the water bearer brought him.
For centuries he has watered my dreams
and not asked for repayment or kiss.
I therefore now give him the mystic rose.

It is a redder facsimile of my heart
which is still out there in the snow,
but which I think is ready to come home
before a scarlet tanager or some such
temperate bird, a jackdaw or warbler,
decides that it is red suet.

Song of Heart Returning

In or out of body
In memory
In dreams
You are rose heart.

Wild heart
The potter's apprentice
The singer of praise
Handmaid of the ancient
Of days

Look no more outside yourself
Sings my heart returning.

A Quartet of Daffodils

I think it must be spring
because yesterday morning on Spadina
there was an Indian woman walking
wrapped in maximum eight yards of sari cloth.
It was sheer and a luminous color
like the nectar of pressed apricots.

A red dot punctuated the center of her brow,
like a small and urgent point of energy
had found its way to the surface of her skin,
and jeweled or a drop of blood, it was gleaming.
I think it must be spring because
there is not a host but a quartet of daffodils

sprung up in the front yard of Gore Vale.
They stand not straight but bowed over so.
I think that they had a hard time making it out
of their frozen birthplace inside the earth.
Nevertheless, they are here and have come in first.
The runners-up are the crocuses.

But the evergreen never went under,
it just spread its branches taut and took the worst
that winter had to offer. Do not go under
and one day you may be crowned with evergreen.
This year is my third spring, the third time
that I have been witness to the cycle of the seasons.

Where I am born, there is no such thing,
seasons just shift over a bit to accommodate
the one following. Our winters bring tangerines
and pimento winds. Bless now death, resurrection,
the peculiar ascension of ice falls finally away.

I think it must be spring now because today
I feel so tender, like all early things budding.
And even if I am coming in exhausted,
bowed, bent, drawn, and yellow-skinned
like my very first quartet of daffodils
I know now that this is undeniably spring.

Coo Coo

Coo coo, fool fool.
Hear what that old man bird with the rusty chesnut belly
and gutteral call rasps at you. He is declaring you fool fool.

From the Parakeet in the garden that Simon Peter heard
to the parson Johncrow with the distinguishing white feather,

the little grass quit and the quit with yellow shoulder
all of them feel they can jump up and dub you, fool fool.

Ringillidae finch, chattering sparrows and grosbeaks,
follow-line birds of dull plumage who nest in cavities

and eat of accumulated insect droppings, convene conference
to discuss what they term your extraordinary appearance.

How you appeared first as ground dove taking low, observing how
the scissor-tail hummingbird cut through gravity and accomplished

flight mastery. Fly backwards or straight ahead and even hover,
winged helicopter, on the same spot when mark time is needed.

They write you off as birdbrain when you were trying to fly
and the killy and hawk and the mockingbirds laughed at you.

Your father himself, wise as pattoo, took you to one side
and whispered, "Do not be overfriendly with the John Crow family."

What made you ignore him and decide to fly with vultures,
chicken-hawks, back-stabbing petchary and carrion-eating company?

Rufoustal flycatcher big Tom fool, his litle brother, sad flycatcher
little Tom Fool, want to come and duck their muddy heads.

O cavity dwellers laying heavily spotted eggs (and want to call them
poems). Even they feel that they can call you fool fool.

Once you imitated the Sarah bird and lived in the hills in search
of elevation, frequented forests and made your nest feather-lined

but you lacked the necessary steel gray plumage to be of the tyrant
flycatcher kind. So you dropped down to the plains to regroup.

And dance bird, Ivy Baxter told you that Xamayca is a land older
than most, that it is in fact a pointed finger, a raised shoulder

of Atlantis under the sea, where twenty billion drowned birds
and drowned dreams lie, with lost poets, sing sad aye coo coo.

You need to know that you are of the species Trochilidae,
and if you live content to be ground dove and come-follow-me

and choose for confidantes labba mouth sharp-billed kestrels
and fire hawks, why wonder that your emerald plumage is singed?

So once more, Trochilidae of the family of 319 species, you have
ranged from far Alaska to the sheer heights of the Andes

where you fly in the form of wide-winged cousin to condor
and small up yourself over Cuba as Ave, size of a bumblebee.

Bill and tongue, tongue and bill, upcurved, downcurved, slender, slim
sight up your sign, the half moon sickle with the fixed star within.

Bill of sword which will cut through sword of treacherous king.
Bill to gather, such a gathering, of noisome insects self-promoting.

Gather nettles, then turn to draw the sweet honey nectar, gather
nectar and eat insects too, the sweet and the bitter both nourish you.

Dazzle and dazzle them, wear your garments iridescent like flying
precious stones. Aye sapphire, and topaz in flight and emerald lustre

to astonish and illuminate. When they gather to study your vocal
chords in order to imitate your taffeta laugh, make the percussive

click and sound the Om, with the whir-beating of your wings.
Flash and fly when the swarms of wannabees come, it is meet

to lower your body's temperature and draw down into your
necessary reserve, there to go silent till the sun stuns them

with the gold of enlightenment. Who except Farid'du din Attar,
The Rose's essence, can call you to conference and Parliament?

Bringing the Wild Woman Indoors

You'd cleansed yourself with astringent blue soap lather
rinsed your skin in a baptism of pure rainwater

robed yourself in starched garments of white
turned your face upward to catch the light

and then she came in. Disheveled and weeping,
her hair tangled, her half-hemmed dress trailing.

She had mauve-stained shadows under her eyes
like the solitaire had brushed its wings there all night.

"Instead of an attic," she says, "you have forced me to live
under the house-bottom with your discarded things.

Me, the one who stood sentinel outside your doorway
while you cultured the new voice, the new poetry.

Who was it ripped the face off the devil when
he tried to petrify you down in the stone gardens?

I am the one who masked for you for years so
they believed that you were half-witted and slow

and because of that they chat you, laughed at you
and left you alone, allowing you to decode the news

brought by the viridian-plumaged bird who flew down
at night from the Ashanti aviary in Nanny Town."

And as she spoke you saw yourself in her, the wild woman,
your true sister. And you say, "Thank you for being the mad one,

the wild heart, the crazy woman, the Accompong Nanny warrior."
And that's when you brought her to live inside with you forever.

The Revival Song of the Wild Woman

The wild woman will never let you go back to living alone.
She has you in her control, leading you hopelessly astray,
preaching her don't-care philosophy, "No matter what the people
of the world may say."

And she tells you now to go with her to where our music is buried,
and sing loud revival songs that will waken the dead
singers and players of instruments who sell out Don Drummond
and Bob Marley's heritage.

This morning she caught your attention early, told you to dress
in fiery red, and you who have been keeping your life colors
in the range between muted and pastel are now garbed
in brimstone red

with an infinite number of polka dot eyes all over so you
are now able to see behind, before, above and all around you.
And she is telling you to take a bus up to August Town to where
Alexander Bedward dipped them.

And she says that you are to throw stones in Hope River and trouble
the water, to signal the time of the coming of a new shepherd. Then
take a country bus down to Half Way Tree and go and stand
by the fountain.

There you are to testify freely and not worry what your enemies say,
for they will never live long enough to vanquish you, therefore do
your unconquered dance right there, your dance of David trump
and wheel o' rock steady

accompanied by tumbling tamborines and a funde drum and a kete
drum and a silver horn to blow the bad-minded down. Yes,
the wild woman is in ascendancy today, summoning the freed soul
in you to testify and pray.

To wear brimstone red and to wrap your head and to move seamlessly
up and down between the worlds of spirit and sense, like the flight
of the mystical dove. And if your mother won't come, and if your
father won't come

Peace and Love I leave with you, Peace and Love,
and if your mother won't come, and if your father won't come
Peace and Love I leave with you, Peace and Love.

Aye Spring

Aye Spring, you broke your promise again,
said that this time you were here to stay
now here you send winter in your place.

You, my capricious one, leave me no choice
but to return to my rock, rock steady.
I bolt the door and draw the blinds

and trump around the sacred stone,
holy ground the space of my room becomes
as I rock and wheel and wheel and turn.

See how I turn and turn past all betrayals
past promises broken I turn my roll.
I am one with the circular motion of the world.

So St. Francis of Assisi wheeled, so did
Jalal Ud Din Rumi, Rex Nettleford and Mirabai.
All the righteous ones wheel around

the cosmic sun. Wheel away the weights
pulling at the hems, the love bush and remora,
the haul and pull of land and water,

wheel me so I rise above false promises
and see spring's perfidy with the eyes of the heart.
Make it come when it will come. Till then, I dance.

Close to You Now

Close to you now
I talk at the evening sky.
Maybe that is where your heart is,
your chest all decorated with stars
and the keen scythe blade
of the crescent moon.

Ever since I gave up telling to anyone
but you, I have become so filled
with love that I used to waste.
Now I confess to you straight.
I ask you questions. I sleep.
I speak the answers when I wake.

When I gave up walking
from door to door with my begging bowl
I became conscious that my bowl
had been always full of the fine gold wheat
which only the prayerful can see and eat.
And all the time I was living on leftovers.

I lie in my bed and cry out to you.
I cover myself with a humming tune spread
which says as it weaves itself
you, you and only you.
No one could ever sight up
the true intentions of this heart.

But ever since I stop explaining
I watch them blow past me like chaff.
Alone and silent now I hear again
the coded notes played by the rain
which dictated the first poems.
I want to walk across this green island

singing like the Guinea woman
showers, showers of blessing
until you cover my lips
and I go silent and still
and I will see your face
and want then for nothing.

Illinois Poetry Series
Laurence Lieberman, Editor

The Ways We Touch
Miller Williams (1997)

The Rooster Mask
Henry Hart (1998)

The Trouble-Making Finch
Len Roberts (1998)

Grazing
Ira Sadoff (1998)

Turn Thanks
Lorna Goodison (1999)

Traveling Light:
Collected and New Poems
David Wagoner (1999)

Some Jazz a While:
Collected Poems
Miller Williams (1999)

National Poetry Series

Eroding Witness
Nathaniel Mackey (1985)
Selected by Michael S. Harper

Palladium
Alice Fulton (1986)
Selected by Mark Strand

Cities in Motion
Sylvia Moss (1987)
Selected by Derek Walcott

The Hand of God and a Few
Bright Flowers
William Olsen (1988)
Selected by David Wagoner

The Great Bird of Love
Paul Zimmer (1989)
Selected by William Stafford

Stubborn
Roland Flint (1990)
Selected by Dave Smith

The Surface
Laura Mullen (1991)
Selected by C. K. Williams

The Dig
Lynn Emanuel (1992)
Selected by Gerald Stern

My Alexandria
Mark Doty (1993)
Selected by Philip Levine

The High Road to Taos
Martin Edmunds (1994)
Selected by Donald Hall

Theater of Animals
Samn Stockwell (1995)
Selected by Louise Glück

The Broken World
Marcus Cafagña (1996)
Selected by Yusef Komunyakaa

Nine Skies
A. V. Christie (1997)
Selected by Sandra McPherson

Lost Wax
Heather Ramsdell (1998)
Selected by James Tate

So Often the Pitcher Goes to Water
until It Breaks
Rigoberto González (1999)
Selected by Ai

Other Poetry Volumes

Local Men and *Domains*
James Whitehead (1987)

Her Soul beneath the Bone:
Women's Poetry on Breast Cancer
Edited by Leatrice Lifshitz (1988)

Days from a Dream Almanac
Dennis Tedlock (1990)

Working Classics:
Poems on Industrial Life
Edited by Peter Oresick and
Nicholas Coles (1990)

Hummers, Knucklers, and Slow
Curves: Contemporary Baseball Poems
Edited by Don Johnson (1991)

The Double Reckoning of
Christopher Columbus
Barbara Helfgott Hyett (1992)

Selected Poems
Jean Garrigue (1992)

New and Selected Poems, 1962–92
Laurence Lieberman (1993)

The Dig and *Hotel Fiesta*
Lynn Emanuel (1994)

For a Living: The Poetry of Work
Edited by Nicholas Coles and
Peter Oresick (1995)

The Tracks We Leave:
Poems on Endangered Wildlife
of North America
Barbara Helfgott Hyett (1996)

Peasants Wake for Fellini's *Casanova*
and Other Poems
Andrea Zanzotto; edited and translated
by John P. Welle and Ruth Feldman;
drawings by Federico Fellini and
Augusto Murer (1997)

Moon in a Mason Jar and
What My Father Believed
Robert Wrigley (1997)

The Wild Card: Selected Poems,
Early and Late
Karl Shapiro; edited by Stanley Kunitz
and David Ignatow (1998)

Typeset in 10.5/13 Apollo
with Helvetica Neue Extended display
Designed by Paula Newcomb
Composed by Jim Proefrock
at the University of Illinois Press
Manufactured by Cushing-Malloy, Inc.